47074

1

British Columbia

Photographs by Paul von Baich

Introduction by Robert Harlow

Toronto
OXFORD UNIVERSITY PRESS
1979

2

3

Designed by FORTUNATO AGLIALORO

© Oxford University Press (Canadian Branch) 1979
ISBN 0-19-540303-7
1234-2109
Printed in Hong Kong by
EVERBEST PRINTING COMPANY LIMITED

Introduction

There has always been a tendency for people from elsewhere to think of British Columbia as the city of Vancouver and environs. There are good reasons. Not only does half the population of B.C. live in that two or three per cent of the province's land-area, but also some of our most awesome scenery lies within an hour's travel from the centre of the city. The valley and the delta of the Fraser River are there, the coast mountains, the sea, and an incredible array of islands, for which this coast is famous. Probably few places on earth are so astoundingly and concentratedly blessed with land- and sea-scapes as the southwest corner of B.C.

Still, for all its variety and beauty, and for all the ambience of its lifestyle, the lower left-hand corner of the province is not British Columbia. B.C. is an immense piece of geography—better than half a million square kilometres—big enough to encompass the whole of the west coast of the USA from the 49th parallel to Mexico and from the Rockies to the sea; or Great Britain and Ireland, with enough left over for a good number of Chilcotin ranches. And inside its borders lie as many terrains as much of the rest of the world offers. It has lakes—in the Nation Chain, for instance—150-200 km long; the valleys of the Skeena, Peace, Fraser, Thompson and Columbia; that great high and ancient lava cap known as the Chilcotin; a flowering desert down the whole length of the Okanagan's lakes; ice fields; hot springs ... But enough. This is not a tourist promotion. What I want to do is suggest—as an introduction to von Baich's extraordinary photographs—that nature's plan for B.C. was quite simply to create an impregnable wilderness. Not a teeming one like the Amazon, or a frozen and forbidding one like the roof-of-the-world, Tibet, but a unique one; a wilderness not empty, certainly uncrowded and unhurried, but also immensely *sane,* unlike the neurotic African and South American jungles or the permanently tranquilized wastes at the poles or in the hinterlands of the Pamirs.

Man has had difficulty with B.C. The wilderness has resisted penetration. Polynesians drifted or paddled here and found the coastal islands were Edens where a family could live in its own cove on a cedar raft during the summer and harvest salmon and shellfish from the sea, and berries and meat from the shore. But there was little penetration into the interior, and many of the tribes that made the trek across the Bering Strait between Siberia and Alaska wisely headed for the open prairies and southward towards Mexico. The B.C. wilderness held nearly fast. 175 years ago the first white man arrived. 120 years ago there was a gold rush up the long gut of the Fraser. 100 years ago Gassy Jack Dayton's peers began to build a town that was soon to be called Vancouver—and they stayed: Burrard Inlet, it appears, fostered an extension of the cove culture the first natives of the coast had established. It is not hard, metaphorically, to think of Vancouver as floating calm and protected from the sea at its front door and the continental climate at its back, and living off the bounty of the ocean and the land.

But 'upcountry', where about a third of the population lives, life is quite different. There are small cities—Prince George, Kamloops, Kelowna—and settlements that have toughed it out for half or three-quarters of a century—Nelson, Merritt, Revelstoke; there are places that are simply lumber or oil and gas towns—Houston and Fort St John; and there are places where people just live or come into to shop—like McBride or Greenwood or 100 Mile House. And in all these places there is still a sense of hanging on.

The wilderness is there just beyond the last street. It is a constant in von Baich's vision of British Columbia, as you will see from looking at his pictures in this book. It is there as a backdrop even to a cityscape. It is at the edges of his seascapes. Rivers tear a rock-edged trench through it. Occasionally muskeg forces it to retreat to the edge of a northern valley. Sometimes a totem pole uses it and gives it human shape, or a ranch home or church sits in a clearing threatened by it. Often the wilderness itself is the subject of von Baich's photographs: it is simply *there*. Jungle. We here in B.C. seldom think of it as jungle, but that's what it is. There is the rain-forest jungle of Vancouver Island and the coast of the mainland, and there are half a million square kilometres of spruce, hemlock, pine, and fir, far upcountry, that are jungle too. Von Baich's photographs confirm this: one doesn't simply look at them, one is forced to watch them, expecting movement there in the wilderness, just where the frame cuts across the image.

We who are natives of B.C. are more often than not impatient with our wilderness—something von Baich senses—but we shouldn't be. Our towns and cities look like any other towns and cities, supplied as they are with rubber-stamp designs and multinational products. But our wilderness is not only unique in the world, it is romantic and precious beyond belief. Unfortunately we culturally oppressed Canadians will not know and understand these things viscerally until the rest of the world recognizes them and celebrates them for us.

Perhaps by then it will be too late, because if the white man had a hard time penetrating the wilderness, he has now developed

technology which, in the last generation, has laid the dead hand of
progress against the pulse of the life that has existed here from the
beginning. Surely compromises must be made: people must live. But if
rational choices are not made soon, the wilderness that will return to
take over the land after it has been exploited will not be the one
celebrated in this book, but of a different kind, whose reality elsewhere
people visit British Columbia to escape. Von Baich does not here often
photograph people, but those few he has portrayed have about them
the spirit necessary to live with the wilderness. Watch for a while his
young back-to-land couple—whose beauty is alive, palpable—or his
few wilderness men, and you may begin, as I did once more, to
understand what the land is demanding: not that we live constantly
challenged by its wilderness, but that we co-operate with it, know its
ultimate strength and its true worth.

This book contains much fine photography, and much good pictorial
information about B.C., but beyond that it suggests a reality that gives
depth and worth to the image that has always been British Columbia's
from its beginnings. It is a book for those who live here as well as for
people elsewhere; for those who have, perhaps, given up their
wilderness, or had it taken from them. I have favourite images I've
claimed for my own: the seascape at sunset with fishboats in the
foreground; the solemn simple face von Baich has extracted from a
totem pole; the aerial study of the river meandering through a long
northern muskeg swamp; a town at evening holding its own at the
mouth of a mountain pass; a bear caught against the side of a hill by
the first snowfall of the season. It feels good to know that this is home
for me, and still a place for all of us for all seasons.

List of Plates

4   5

9

10

12

13

14   15

16

18

19

23

24

28

29

30

31

37

39

42　　43

44

45

47

49

50

51

52

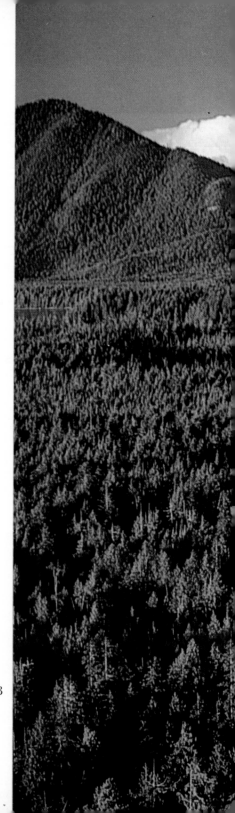

53

54

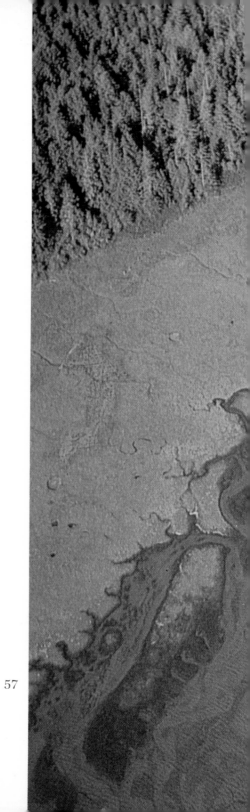

56   57

70 71

74

76

81

83

84